THE SELECTED POEMS OF STEVE CAREY

The Selected Poems of Steve Carey
© Estate of Steve Carey, Marion Farrier, executor, 2009

All Rights Reserved
ISBN-13: 978-1-930068-42-1
ISBN-10: 1-930068-42-5

Library of Congress Control Number: 2009927522

Subpress books are available from Small Press Distribution.
1341 Seventh Street
Berkeley, CA 94710-1409
www.spdbooks.org

Selected for subpress by Anselm Berrigan
Book design and typesetting by Anna Moschovakis
Cover art by Jonathan Allen
Photo of Steve Carey by Unknown
Printed by Bookmobile

THE SELECTED POEMS OF STEVE CAREY

edited by
Edmund Berrigan

CONTENTS

Finding a copy of any of Steve Carey's seven books these days amounts to finding and ransacking the book collection of one of his friends. A few years ago Bill Berkson, publisher of Big Sky Press, found a box of *Gentle Subsidy*, Carey's longest book, and made it available through Small Press Distribution. I found a copy, surprisingly, of *Smith Going Backward*, Carey's chapbook copyrighted in 1968, at a used bookstore in Williamsburg, New York City a couple years ago—the back story being that a publisher and collector of poetry had unloaded a large portion of his library there. *The California Papers*, published by United Artists in 1981, is still somewhat available, as perhaps is *AP*, published by Archipelago Books in 1984. The other three "books" didn't have a spine, and are probably difficult to locate among one's own book collection, let alone anywhere else.

Carey began publishing in the 60s with *Smith Going Backward*, a chapbook of short poems. *AP* and *The California Papers* were both initially composed in the 60s, but remained unpublished until the 80s. The former a long open field work, the first two sections included here; the latter a prose-ish work that also includes several pages of quatrains, which Carey included in *Gentle Subsidy*, and which is also included here. "Fleur-de-Lis," a very airy poem, was published as an issue of *Blue Suede Shoes*, a magazine co-edited by Keith Abbott and Carey.

Gentle Subsidy, published by Bill Berkson's Big Sky Press in the mid-70s, has the healthiest representation of Carey's poems: enthusiastic, with a hint of Philip Whalen influence. Steve's other book in the 70s, *The Lily of St. Mark's*, was another fugitive publication by Ted Berrigan's then occasionally resurrected "C" press, coming out in 1978. 1987's *20 Poems*, published by Unimproved Editions and republished (again, bound in glorious staples) by Open 24 Hours press in 2006, was Steve's last book. Those poems retain Carey's "Old Enthusiast" voice: the large man with a sweet deep growl of a voice telling great stories or announcing favorite phrases. A number of the poems are pieced together from television dialogue, another two are catalogues of phrases, including the eminently readable "The Complaint: What Are You Some Kind Of".

Steve Carey died of a heart attack in 1989, at the age of 43. Nearly 20 years later, here is a chance for a new generation to discover the pleasure in reading Carey's poetry. These poems are terrific to read out loud, and meant to be heard. They are a selection from Steve's life work. Welcome to them.

Edmund Berrigan
New York, 2009

THE SELECTED POEMS OF STEVE CAREY

THE OLD ENTHUSIAST

Doubts of plastic certainty—age and wisdom—
an automatic ivy one of many reasonable shades
trucking its applicability and mouthing hands
far over the horizon at the farthest fence and morning—
never memorable in a mirror or a shadow
but possibly summoned by surprise in a similar dying
sometime that day.

The constantly new darks.

Later—life by a sea you can't live in,
and a death neglecting the tutored heart
                                        Where is it?—
and the entire congregation ceases in its seats at once,
                            some looking.

Here comes the echo—an accusation.
The question itself is evidence—
the slogan is lifted, you see, from its dilemma
                            and taken as contribution.

Sleep, it seems constantly there,
like a pocket or childhood impervious to brown
and the day-long sunsets it inherits
                                    no matter the weather
nor the real complaints.

You are the journal of yourself—dying—
spending not indulging, trying not alive;
you think, you sense, you feel—everything matters!—
you do so much—and then you go to bed again.

"LIFE IN A NORTHERN TOWN"

Six in the morning, outside
Blowing snow in the perfect dark, 22°
I'm awake after awakening dreams
(Often happens just before dawn)
Marion and Joe abed asleep
Joe wearing his earphones, radio going
I put them on, pour a glass of juice
Get some coffee going
Come out here in skivvies to write this
Loving them both so in a northern town

PHILIP WHALEN WE LOVE YOU COME HOME!

Then the marigolds (there are
No marigolds, I'm betting) remind me
Of paint, a war of paint what a war!
Like a city

        Can a park
(Not an ultimatum) be a reprieve? not a suggestion?
In such a city? not an ultimatum?
Sure
Can you possibly avoid thinking "green"?

"Aster on your fence your marish marl
It's aster"

Same thing

What a city! What a park!

What a   bush what a baby!

I ran into no one
Outside the de Young the JAPANESE
ART FESTIVAL

        Painting
Ceramics and sculpture through February 19

STAGGERLEE

The distance, with its apotheosis part, "glass,"
is come to hover permanent
in the weather between the bells
in all the fountains....

He did not finish the report.

Stance and hands, nude of cue, both
went to speculate, and did,
as, too, this becomes the time
that wall enrolled an edge.

The place capitulated.
A disaster of feathers grew and, in a word,
surrounded the bone.
He threw a little radio at the window,
wrecking the site—for a sec.

Fuck.

Avid as that space, then, he took
the candor of the farm as his own,
but bearing a notion of surrounding data,
"feathers," winking with feeling
whether construed weeping, as from hegemony,
or the conduct of the accidents themselves.

Death, for instance, in its various proof,
surprised home at the theory, although
"the rest departed" was how it went
in some perimeters.

The setting turned into an arrow, or (again),
a "set," and a new duty
swayed over the end of mail.

...vast, amazing...

First, a storm, then the heat, were each
outflanked as, say, by statuary. True,
he was barefooted; but false he was
ever so omitted. Nor would he
once award a moment, tag it "floating"
if he could, for every fear
the next was then "on deck"
and (he told me) wrong.

This would be the day...his first without
mention of its movement.
Duck down, duck down, darry darry down,
he was singing.

He was at the root—hardly under—wasn't he...
where it is a kind of cave of the good, weird,
is testament he can travel in the version
of what returns to die at a center.

Ghost proposals, which he later named a chapter,
of rewards of nowhere without gardens
and the like, broke rank constantly
to outshout mandates for the crowding
of other arms and legs—shush!—
with waves of other pressures, facts in tents.

It was apparent:
They have no time for down below.

He is distressed. Winds, he sees,
closed to throbbing, flip away
in daily accounts of "me," "me," "me,"—
Staggerlee.

THE AMERICAN TUB

The birds are really something, so's the grey
the belt of freeway its sound
                                        constantly telling of my absence
which is a lie so terrific I have to go to the bathroom
When I think of it I am thinking of a mouth
                                        surrounded in grey
so actual and so impossible like the birds which like the freeway
I can never

                    It's a confusion without a bit of dizziness, not knowing
beyond ice what you used to like or
doing exactly what you said you couldn't (wouldn't) exactly the way
you said you couldn't
all over everything
                                and then shopping or talking about being hot
It's then you know anything could be dire
                                        but it isn't
You're a great American for inventing a pleasure that doesn't hurt
tho you still had to talk about one that did

                                        So did I
I am Steve Carey, you're Cindy Reidel
                                        and we are waiting for nothing
so familiar as what we don't call ourselves but almost
                                                    zip zip
So at the risk of sounding finicky I'll say
                                        landing isn't enough for arrival
but it's really something to arrive here once you have
and four buses later I was naked in the grey
                                        singing "Oh-no-no-no-yah"
a fallible other
            who won't (it's starting to work) knock

so nicely

So the myth has risks too which is why I
I don't remember and don't care (it works!)
I hear
the helicopter over the belt reporting
the grape juice is cold and fine and the grey has a sun in its middle
or did
and birds, something is on your lip
and I want to own that too
Jesus

I haven't got the money to get back
and it feels like this my last cigarette over the hill from you
where there's nothing but houses all around me
and the fear of dying of shark
any time we like

I am trying to be utter
I am trying to be like the music
which hates me and which I don't know how to like nevertheless
You're swacked
in honor of what you like however
I'm either glad or wish it was me

SMITH GOING BACKWARD

What terrible fine delight
The indicator, timeliness and its end
Givens and in moods strange as a fictional doctor
Moss crotches of oak and acacia

I was safe as an apology, that dependable
So (among other things) you couldn't
Have been there. No one could have

I'd no need for imagining your sheltering grove
The sky got so black had I been in a movie
(And I was) anyone had they been there
(And you weren't!) might have seen

But I had no need for imagining
No you and no I, and neither one of us
Masturbated on that hill and tree
In that damp like you say. Tho yes
I can easily see it now, along with
And because of your fears—mess halls
Masterpieces, weddings and me
Do as I do and do not. Do it on everything

JULIA

If the avoidances of probability are so sonorous
(the nerves are there it's just harder) then
hemming is only consequence (it hurts) in pants
(and because you know it will be disappointing
you know it will happen (the moon sifts the promises
of habit) (is it July? Retreat to the general
—packaging, shade)) (soon the open windows will find
their place and thru them a browning garden
of inclination will pass veiled in brand names
—the saucers of foreseen sleep or sex) improbable
and very clear, enjoying herself on the sane
it doesn't hurt and the only time she stands is
when she can be a part of the horizon wet
without pants or nowhere with friends, volleyballs

LOVE FOR THE LYING

Something of mine in the soup cup
An impersonation cloistering me
And on the street corner of paisley vaginas
I am a paisley vagina softly denying it

Stereophonic the smells
"I'll say it: highly you"
Highly me as the days move away from my birthday
I am that much more lost in a koan of the compass

Off the corner
And in an intersection with a whistle
While (tho I don't know them) all I desire
Throw stones at the lights
"Honk! The truck of no frustration
What pomp directionless device!"

Or next monotonous

Or next infatuated every kiss my first

We are all naked as possible
Not knowing who is wool in the embracing tub
A pile of smoldering peat in the drug store
We blame it on the coffee, go home

Tonight we know it's name we gave us
Another ridiculous ignition, smoke without fire
"Forget it"

When I think we've changed I'm afraid to say a word
And when I do it isn't me at all

36

Putting all these people to clause
How come?
Elinor D'arcy shall I ransom you
from your airplane, your paragraph?
(Home, and much to Frieda's disgust
she refuses the air conditioning
Makes her feel (ha!) like
she's in an airplane) Ha!

Elinor's impending tizzy

It will smell cold and willful, I think
An intersectioned iceberg trying
to pull itself together
manipulating cross currents like cubes in a glass
(Boom) They forgot
how big the ocean was
Boom
They forgot how big they were
7/8ths or something in somebody else's glass

Say, I wish your name were Julia
What a book that was! what a face!
How come?

FOR MY LADY THE BEGINNING IS IMMENSE AND LONELY

We die to choose who!

Hotels move in our heads.
Under the news—complaints, always
(By which, incidentally, apocalypse is kept
Unsensed without a ramp).

You, choosing me,
Light the merit penmanship, love-certainty—
Age, brittleness, ivy, snow,
What have you.

Do not sneer at this. Me certain.
The unable mirror never pushed light
That summoned, or that special;
Every way I turn, arms burst their darks.

A suitcase, remember, means "for life,"
As in "that day" (or camp).

Details in New York

You will carry it uptown, this journal:
A frenzied hour in the penmanship
Of a while, or, and your surprise.

JOE HILL

You think so

Odds are

Six years of fencing lessons
that you might walk into a room—
on camera and off—properly
and at least once perfectly—
down the crapper

The sudden sense that
all your life has been only preparation
for this moment
in this car
at this intersection
this afternoon
waiting for the light to change

Alternately, maybe you just know
you're going to die today
and just barely don't realize it

The weather gets quickly heavy
or the forecast does

Rooms (cars) are rife—
ripe–
with portent

Ripe

"I never died," said he
"How are you?
How're you doing?"

MEDICAMENTOSA

Thank you, bones!

I fit everywhere
and you fit everywhere.

Blind blood will answer
the gloved applause.

Trust me.

AFTER LI PO (AFTER ALICE NOTLEY)

Running dust, a light morning rain
Dark wet dust on window sills, freshened brickwork
Outside the city just awake
You call for another cup of coffee while I'm up
Well, old friend, I called you in from this storm
Leaving, please remember, that I too start soon
For this little alley in San Francisco
back of the Southern Pacific station at Third and Townsend
in redbrick of drowsy lazy afternoon

A MENU

Tracing watermarks that there or not
May or may not make a difference
A girl removed, impenetrable
As a stain, a window of night
Curtained in too much talk
I have been here much too long

"…hardly what I meant but shut up"

Later flushed in Jello and tea
Fouled in hair and an ouch
There is a sudden faith in presentiment
A wish for first persons without lips

The blinds drill and bite the
Initial is recurring
Something cold and delicious in that belly too

GENTLE SUBSIDY

for Cindy Arkin

So many poems,
started then neglected...

Rites to favors, small and sudden
necessities, dim, never certainly
of a nature, elemental or my own—

And none of which, or almost,
previous—the poems before—
in lines to lights of hasty
but that standard, earlier neglect:

The ash fallen off the cigarette
in the hand flipped at the wrist
after the fly, corner of the table, by the light

You get the idea

(Me and my absences...

After months, a continent (both ways),
a wife, the friends and then the seasons
whose absences (see!) never fail
to remind me of each other, entirely,
and most often back and forth)

In fact, if I'm not mistaken,
somewhere up this page, near the top
somewhere—(too soon, it was, for an example)—
this pen was *completely* the wrong size

(Nothing is more naked-feeling
than dressing in your own examples)
(Brrrr)

But—to get back—
so what, I say,
said...and the pen, its size
and so on, moved on

This is that page

And screw too that feeling
being so naked only
in my own examples.
It's all telling.
And my friends, I'm sure,
have many more and far better
ones too

No matter how, I'm all here

No matter how long, I always
would have been

Just as happy, just as glad...

But then, I knew
I wouldn't write another poem
until I was in love again

LAS PALMAS

Sick chocolate Tuesday, Wednesday, haze, next month
it'll be just like this only hot and I won't
be sick I won't be sick

                           An accident in the airborn air

                                           hear that clock?
and old lemonade, nothing to swallow, pay attention
Here I am

               I am watching the new rainbow
in color remote control

                     just as I dreamt it
pouring coffee over a toothache, four seconds, a dream
and there'll be no more elegant fits

                         give up
let's be calm, right, the glass-door-stop
incidental and perfect

               here I come
the radio bitching, the heat no longer needed but there

                                 amidst the shades
where we are dutifully surprised by it sure we'll be surprised
this is it, the beach, THIS IS IT

                     stop the car
hear that ocean?

           quick
hear it?

         I'm not sick I never was

                    toxins toxins
the lemonade, the sky, your smile, the conches

                         all pink now
"That's what I'm like"

               and *that's*
what Coty Originals   is about

NEW PETIT MAL

Getting out of bed one day one is deaf and therefore
Discovered with the message your leg simply has to tell me
Start to finish every morning of the world.

                                                The bones—too frail—
Suggest to the veteran Frenchman remains of a place of fire
Left and belted into a kind of eggshell or crabshell...
But as I know where the drawings blossom
Just as I know the bells that chime for the recent dead—
Baby-white panics from the tower tops
Filling and fleeing the four-way sky
Which would be struck midflight.

But they are there
                    riding deficient wings
Under trees
             through the park.

I cup my hands
                waiting for their buff feathers—

A gargle of bones
                down through the scrub

FAMES AWAY

Furious machines, difficult objects, dilapidate
The little horizon appearances
Of middle meanings (not communications)

Too large for noise afterall
The first, in sooty residence
Drums inaudibly

Semblance of the sun
Shuffling on foot, springing and inevitable
Lightly, a larger audience

One responsive fact, exactest at it
Naked, festival sphere
What it is being

Alive with the view and the birds
Repetition never quite clear of uncertainty
Luminous vassals beyond

Rounding, "O," the motive, changes
On infant legs the spirit's weight
Its noon included, roundabout

Throughout space. On the edge—
And through included—merely visible—
The fish, pensive, in reeds

The cataracts, ruddy hammer, red, blue
The hard sound, its distances, solid
The moment, rain, the sharp flesh

Coming on the habits, nakedness
To nakedness, the high, arrogant
Night air, now in mind

BLACK AND WHITE

And this is supposed to the happiest
        day in a woman's life! Why won't
London answer? Five million dollars!?
        We haven't even begun to fight!
Where is he? Last we heard one of the girls here got
        a postcard from Singapore. It would
be just like that guy to die at a time like
        this. No? Breakfast can wait.
Let bygones be bygones. Table for one please.
        Table for two. Who does she think
she is? Wait a minute! That's it. *The Star*
        calls her a husband stealer...
She denies it. The things I've taken
        from that newspaper. You want
me to kill myself. If you don't want to marry me just say so.
        I'm sorry, I've nothing to say. Let go of me!
Oh, honey, I want to meet
        the man who saved your life this morning.
Sorry...I'm afraid I wasn't concentrating
        Shall we sit down? Remember me?
Goodbye. Cocktails? In my state room
        at 7:00? There's only one hitch. Why, he's
like a brother. Not *my* brother!
        I've lost the key. Hello? Hurry up! You mean
that key was there all night?
        All talk. I'll get it. Give the gentleman
a cigar. Perfect, sir! Ah, this
        is what makes life worth living. If he's
first class I'll travel steerage.
        I take it all back...
He's good. What do you think?
        I'm asking you to marry me. Afraid I'll

make a scene, huh? On the contrary.

Leave us join hands. We're off to the races. You wait here. So nice to see you.

He told you all about me? There must be some mistake. What a story!

FOLK SONG

"These reaches." she said, "so blue, gone away."
And offers sweet waters ("if," she says,
"You are asking me") whose quiet lies
Awake through a marked folk who give
"This—no sea of mine," she says.

A need could make the pass
They sicken of, bumping off.
And she says, "I do not let a love bleat
Over losing what was 'sudden' and 'terrible'.
I have no lethal heavens, roaring plenty.
The costs are quick, by rights, here,
And may tear your joy, and sing
Your plans, and sign surprise, and rout
Deep breathing, beef your weaving lean,
And cry, 'Light! Die light! Die light!'"

from AP

Associative Prowess

is what you think of at the end of
                              furious up-all-night
                   checking skies
                     for signs of sunup
          over a glass of ice water, swallowing
                                       more pill
                as the window wins
'Love at Home'
                and all this California
                              "this"
                  follows the Bouncing Ball

You've got to be good
                         you certainly are awake

They seem to be the same
                  on Tuesday, today

        don't they

     when I breathe

                      the WM PENN

            You Suck

                         —Johnny
                               de
                             LA

The streetlights, what can I say?
can't flap the sun back, no

All this determination is ruining my teeth

I have nothing to do with the day

    Elinor thinks it's all in the day before
—my fault—the writer

                    which means (5:something a.m.
                        daylight saving time)

I am afraid of my own ideas
                and sometimes Elinor
    who doesn't even write
              but is my softest idea
    and just full of ideas of her own

    Is she another determination?

What, tho, could be more determined than a suck?

    Which might be why so much life
    has it at its start

        I'm happy about that …
        it a thought too

Reminds me of this idea
gets into the blood sometimes:
              cheap, unsophisticated
a determination for the blood
           singularities
    and no real need for subjects either—

an idea with no place in the brain

An idea in the blood!

Determined without trying

More and more window
a day in motion
with a blue
which is not a march for a blackness
and
two rather natty park bums
walk by for the Safeway trashbins
now before opening

Could anybody stop them?

They aren't trying
they're hungry

I wish I was.

Idea's been in my blood
plenty of times
and never so much as an urge
let alone a real pang or a hardon

Quiet.

It's ten of six

(which poem is this anyway

and the man with the watery voice

(it's the poem in which
that doesn't mean he's gargling

is busy getting ready for work

We wave
(two windows)

and a rash of coffee breaks out over the city
I mean the Greater Los Angeles Area

similarly, the dawn
not down
does do

Off, two friv' and lav' bum fops
nat by for the Safeway trashbin

At ten o'six the man the watery voice gets up
determined to suck me off before work
I steal what I can care about,
get off

But it's up all up sun's up
daylight for the hours
nothing

I can't do anything now
until the mailman comes
Already it's got to be 90 in here
shit
Eat, shit, find a life
(and someone to explain it to)

What's that?
shit!

Dear Philip,

2.

The heat's taken the mint sprouts
David and Phoebe gave us
and burned the shit out of the bird of paradise
already...Two weeks into summer! (Maybe
now, tho, it might not bother to flower.) Ruth's
lawn is good as gone...

Looks like greens are really in for it
The first time, too, I have ever
put them into my life so intentionally like this
    (other way around lots of times)
                               dammit

    So many signals
                    impossible to mourn
–all those cells
              galaxies of them, universes

          down   drying   die

     And (of course) now I notice

Ruth's roses over the arbor
her frantic random front garden
                    bougainvillea in general

      where I live

Luckily there's some cactus here and there

                                    ignoring everything
                        even their own space
                                which they explode.

                        And in back–
banana tree...
                remaining.

Summer.

        There's some others inside the room here
                inside
                                    stalks in pots
            but I can't begin to spell any of them
                (such a nice catalogue too)
                                    (*Basin Greenery*)
All indoors, as I say,
                    and *withering.*
    "It's not the temperature, you know,
it's the poison fucking air it sits here in..."
    Everything goes brown,
after the air,
        the shade of death with a reason,
or a life with one,–
color of a dying
                swindled of titular change and season,
                left–an end that
                                    won't stop, won't clock

                    ***

It's all in the attention.

How my attention adores

                        this bed of window

        where something must break first
        before you get it next.

Is that it?   Nah.

What is a bed to you?
Well, that's what my window is
to my attention
not too infrequently.
Watch this:

            Here comes the mailman
            none too soon

                            He loads up down at the corner there
                            then starts up this side of the street

What a fine handwriting!

        (PAUSE a few seconds; CUT to clock)

        ...Got Nothin'...

Can't think of anything,
                        if not comically so,
that ain't attention.
(Pretty funny, now I come to think of it)

Everything is.

            (not funny (well, maybe)–

what I mean attention)

And so is trust, I have just come to think, everything.

That's 200%

total.

200. Too bad the shades are down now
                                        (105° at least)

or I could enumerate...

It's a war, as I see it,
between temperature and (and) everything else,
            alias attention and trust.

                Tune In Later

It's...
        time to go for more
                        cigarettes and soda.

Should I send this,
                just like this,
                        right the hell to Japan?

Want it?

I don't even know what's in here
And I'll be gone for cigarettes
                    (last chance to mail)
by the time I find out.

                         −a Mysterious Process−

    "Don't forget some more of those cookies."

    "Right."

    (same mystery)

And if I write all about
                    how the weather's raping me
DON'T be telling me it's ALL RIGHT
please
        (and
        thank you)

                    MORE LATER
                    (natch)

Great about all those books of yours.

(You got plants?) (What's dying?)

                                        Love,

                                            Steve

ABOUT POETRY

for Bill Berkson

The laws of love are many
In the dreaming of the book
Which, we hope, includes
Such labors as might assume
Survivors for the song.

Prepagination...The total 'wronged'
Rightful heir's passage—
Ports, harbor, home...the finding
Of his sodden log one day.

Tale go 'way. Remain calypso.
There is herald all in tone.

Trust of the joy of telling.
Trust of the strength
In a subject to be placed
And sustained, hopefully resumed.

The laws of love are many
Times told in the love
Of labor. Stories fall or shy—
The former shade.

"There is, as Chinese novels
Are fond of saying,
'A poem to prove it!'"

Talking in our sleep...
The books grow bigger
And bigger. Fine books.

HOLLYWOOD, SPRING 1924

Zara Vanities, What do they see in each other?
It is the "soon" and "better" got them.
Feeling 'little quicker, new: A drama
Of beautiful women—lilies—who toil not.
But get thin. New thin...Clashing whites...
"Convent bred" in "fuzzy" arbors. Now leading,
Winning, Zara Vanities. Now says never knew fear,
Says "Terror" her last. And here
Is tiny Ina Ansen, the dancer, diving.
Diving into what? Oh, nothing, just diving!

GOT LIVE IF YOU WANT IT

Mick wore a white shirt,
rust-coloured (brownish) suede jacket,
and really stylish modish pants;
tweedish striped in the same rust, black,
and white (background). He wore
flat heeled brown shoes and was
fantastic looking. Brian wore a white shirt
under a red top (*stunning* red against his
golden hair) and beige or white slacks.
Looking at his boots, I'd never noticed
before how small his feet are!
"Keef" wore a regular suit (white shirt)
and boots, and Charlie also
had on a suit with a blue shirt.
Bill wore black slacks, and a leather jacket.

JAPAN

for Philip Whalen

Not a cloud
the sun nothing sudden
a spinster winter a sink full of steam
coming up

Upstairs the man has come back
and the radio is as loud as the shade
bluer
across the street the drum club is stepping
deliberate as airplanes one two three
worth is always local
but I guess it is autumn in that sky too

Letters for nobody, nothing

So do I know the extravagance of space
before I put something in it?
either way I end up chewing it one two fucking three
two minutes fast thought between my it my one
slick twitch across the instep since
Wally coughed he stooped to roar

They have dressed the windows in ambers
and it isn't as late as it feels
anything can be instinct if you try
example me a caramel and I can't drink my tea

PROVIDENCE

for Peg Berrigan

Two different kinds of sleeping aids
(three if you count Jack Daniel's)
(four if you count a boring movie)
and, as I heard a lady say the other day, nada.
Holiday Inn, South Atttleboro, Mass.
with Ted, visiting his mother, ailing,
she's short, a beautiful woman, with what they call
salt and pepper hair, much of her face
in her son. I will kiss that face
twice more. She buried her first love
at 40. Now, at 70, she, her second love,
first born and his friend sit around
a card table, a bottle of Taylor port
and her medical files sliding back and forth
between her son and myself.
(It is not incidental that later on,
talking back at the hotel,
the subject of magic should come up.)

What comes from the heart
is often best shot from the hip...
But, dear God, not always.

OTHER YANKEES

Cold night wind and snow on my back
down 7th street by the park
the day before St. Patrick's Day
singing "...say hello to Marion,"
remembering "I will not faint
in the market." "So what?"

So the long swallow of Cointreau
blooms over the pill in my belly
and salsa music drives up
through the buildings by night
into Marion's new home.
Marion, you're home.

THE COMPLAINT: WHAT ARE YOU, SOME KIND OF

Acturial plight Nostradamus Devil Bat
Overzealous mighty-winged flabbergast
Wholesale heathen plot worry wort
Sci-fi lexicon formenter hassle-free
Quipster of the ring, of the planetary system
Of your choice, of the regrettable necessity
Of your selection, lover of the little village
You choose not to live in, sensationalist (tra-la)
On the wing (tra-la), ever breaded ever-beered contemporary
Of the witless, confessor of regional horrors,
Noxious last-man-in-town-who'd-smite-a-fly,
The delegate slated to spot the pattern,
Overamped readier of the champ, the clue
To all sensory discharge, protean scorn reposed,
A fine thing awry in your youth and others',
Orphan of the phone, TV, stereo, stove, etcetera, yet
Promoter of the hack's activities, duffer's delight,
Haver of your own way, helloer of fortunes,
Traveled-fast hyperbole to hell and gone,
Globe-wide uncle of one, sensational at speed
And sleep, twister of like you did last summer,
Absent weekender, (and) faulty diner
Though deprecating in that, more fortunate
Than unfortunate kin, user of lotions
And marginal balms, believer, muscler in-er,
Frayer, no more than most, of fabulist nerves
In the cause of the fabulous, half-assed fighter
Of the swine, tippler, hoper for the best
While naughty in the tale, puker in the room,
Absolutist, habitual fucker, fucker
Of the young, Halifax (type) charmer, trickster there
In the wind, freezer of you monkeys, incipient whimperer
Of tummyache, any ache, shover of it regardless
Into your pocket, what-the-heller sometimes,

One-time holocaust fortifier, seen murderous Russian
With briefcase, meeter at the park in twenty minutes,
Thinker of something else, mondo tres flagrante,
Endorser, snuffer, in service to the fundament,
Turner, attender, lighter of the candles,
Blower of the candles out, some ugly,
Troublesome divine, lip-quick, occasionally poco loco,
Sucker, oft winter fond, sooth various, humble sinker,
Par considering, comer, turd, a good example,
Known chump, humper, two or three bricks shy of a load,
Thermal crackpot, wishy-wash, twit, object of annual,
Of another, Bahama-bound, neo-passe poontang,
Lunge-monger, thrust-hustler, quasi-objectionable
Quasi-aged quasi-rookie, one of the boys and girls,
Binky, you admit, to your friends, hapless, potentially
Awarded winner, ropey of soul, rank specialist, signifier,
Roiling worm, symptom-listing, self-effulgent, no-show,
Knower of exactly how you feel (really), sleeper, boozer,
Blank-head, some Bub or other, lover, quick-draw, pleaser,
Size-queen or concerned consumer, wondrous in your turn,
Wrong, haunted, fraught, tamed, papacy bewildered,
Someone rarely associated with something (else), yet
A devoted supporter of just that now, one that once
Shook the hand that shook the hand of the one that's sure enough
Now President, sooth-brooder, a fool humid tube, trumpet
To the fluke, reacher, neglectful, fruit-thinker, juiced,
Mourner, bruin-typed, oaf-souled, heavenly described,
Vapid grappler, feeler deeply, bone so, outre,
Vigorous hand washer, resenter of childen or others
Openly fascinated, feckless defendant, drummin' man,
"Fascinatin' Rhythm" whistler, buff, let me
Have a biter, painter of things a certain blue,
Kicker and screamer, squabbler, to this day,
As I say, digger of that crazy beat?

FLIP A COIN

Bereft (little bit), I smile in game time lost
and die the leaded fit
they list under Adverse Reactions
manifested in useful cursing of skyward lifted heads
also little aches that wake the body back
to semblance fortitude, spunk of mate,
deafening (sometimes), choice of smoke,
loss of client, line of fire, of sight,
tons of dough, times of night, chick of sky,
of voice, of ride, of diet, of job,
of departure, of guy, of taste, of great value,
of late, one of the last albeit of the latest, incontinence,
"best of three," change of pants, "make it seven."

THE CALIFORNIA PAPERS

Time passes in the novels it
wouldn't be so bad to puke right
now. the park and me are quits
these wuffing days like shoes

dropped off the bridge rendering
the other (tomorrow) present
(*Season Vs. Sacrifice*—"Interesting!!!")
the winds of their verbs awed and little else

the park cares too. why not
it's like working for the post office
only and get this we deal in
sealed avoidances of mentioned winds

the radios no longer pretend to know
anything. no one does or they'd
die of critical sense. "there goes
your punchline" like that

and that so I moved, memoirs rather
than examples, the anise of those walls
like a clit risen to anonymity
and as the boats relented I tardied

my prologues. a lifetime sidestepping
natural grammar in orgasm. declarative
sentences noon and sundown it's only
been a year so I guess I'm still at it

new fixes on the cortex after
I prove them credible which on my
first visit you did not assume
I landed cumulative in an illusion

of heat so you thought as
my feet too summed the warp
of the stairs bringing news of the
ride over. that was rue round

"hello" which I don't remember
an occasion of the fatality of my
bragging that never did instance
your sampaku suns (there's an awe

you can save us from!) "rolled
out of your pants they did right there
on the steps" I'll be back, I'm young
America! so I have to mention that

brown pool so dumb so momentaneous
and its naught stars mooning in
traditions on the next state. yes I
was back goofing with the map

and am still waiting to be caught at it
it isn't raining and the hibiscus
are Mexico again and I'm twelve
sick and hot. they'd know if I

shut the door so at one
when I wake it's much the initial
blood along with the windows
which still aren't draped

dizziness fit then and many times
still does if it's late and someone
could watch if they belonged in my
intentions or fear that only afterwards

shut it and bit the linen. my
mouth was my hand from then on
my mouth was my mouth and it
reached and at orgasm other bodies

woke and shook their heads a
cute importance whose consequence
was sometimes pleasure so but for
that I moved in incidentals probably

knowing that knowing it made no difference
tho "perhaps" had me breathing into a
paper bag for a year. that's when
I started talking just after love

which still precedes itself. no
nothing. the heat on one side
the sun on the other I'm twenty
I'm ten watching the clock hide behind

the calendar that turns into
a dachshund the instant you
ignore it and your ignorance
the next thing he said cost him

$250,000 I wasn't around for the
trial no by that time I was already
throwing lemons in Carpinteria
more magazines, I had a bell-tower

pockets I was all but back
so later it was possible to
again watch a jamboree dizzy again
and again with their lacks of it

all those movies and all that quickness
if you didn't know it I did that's
when the lights went out. we
coasted home (the library didn't

need me much anyway) tits tits
tits, Philippinos always watering
we never fainted to that-threat did
we and now it's just as impossible

as staying up. I never knew that
part of you it was so much a
part of you, all that energy!
I went right back and did it again

"relax" said the window and explained
everything. don't ever call it home
again. I love you and the next time
I drive for summer you come too

we'll fuck the clock together
zip that fly and it pronounces
your name unwarpable as an absence
"what a meal! it's been two years

since I've had a tomato without
a straw" and five years before that
he pulled down his pants on the A-9
lawn I'm a sonofabitch if he's

not doing it again give me your watch
I want to exercise the eccentricities
of continuum. next was inevitability
available only because it was not

worth mentioning like the mails
up and down the hill, all the neighbors
crazy as Saturday afternoon I was
playing bridge behind my back not yours

I never knew that part of you
it was so much a yah yah yah
tits. "I don't know about you
but to me the most depressing thing

in the world is laying on that
couch watching movies in the middle
of the afternoon" ("he's the guy
wants to kill himself boffing after

lunch") seems I've forgotten why
I'm back you like my letter?
then I didn't know which I wanted
more a smoke or a chocolate

both avoided the bizarre as told
but between them a frightening
comfort was important to upset
and many letters didn't do it

they gutted the church, sunk it
and began fixing the airplanes
it was cool and deliberate you couldn't
speak without electricity so I said

so and waited in my size
watching the man hang TERMINAL
on both sides of the doors
someone must have known before

I did because he gave me pills
I took one and drew up sides
but just before takeoff both went
to the beach and emulated the horizon

all day that's fear but you
can't say it. well I was at
18,000 anyway and counting
"what's that?" it's time no

it isn't, I was returning from
the wrong direction and that's
boredom believed and unnoticed
a riot or a dachshund it was

raining and we were kissing
no one took our picture tho something
big was going on down at the high
school the one that never

forgave you for taking yourself
home neither did I ("that's an
awful lot of gum for five dollars")
so by the weekend it was almost

empty and mine so by Sunday
("but he never shows up in the same
shirt twice") it was theirs and
I moved for a lie for the first time

still unable to sit in lobbies
or enjoy coffee. the sky was glass
and you could hardly stick your
finger in it before they

built a bank on you and everything
went brown. all those shirts!
the hillsides infuriated in sunset
winter smelled like lighterfluid

after all brown as September 28th
and at night I talked in numbers
I never willed me my own metaphor
bullshit. the only way to be natural

is not to know it I tried to be
natural say what I didn't and why
I didn't say kissing the same verb
true but unnatural. such bullshit

not moving because you can't
you can't because you promised
you would said it now you will
or won't. I'd answer anything

if you could ask it now, oh yes
I would! cottage cheese, cookie
a box of raisins. $35 a month
and in every room someone is afraid

of going crazy here's your watch
back better not anticipate me dinner
better not be ready it's a marathon
like love (this is love) I keep thinking

I've lost my place and my ability
for getting away with it and
I have I haven't. "that's an
awful lot of gum for five dollars"

no it isn't. there will never
be another Fourth of July
never another blue doll a
lying Gypsy a lying South African

forget that it isn't that either
(this is love) I called it 2:35
you called it "mine" together it's
called grammar said the sun it

was his night. "what ever happened
to Richard Kolmar?" I guess that
was love the cake we ate it anyway
I couldn't swallow I never can when

I want I have to   nevermind
flight 759 9:15 Thursday
in the meantime I'm not in the
hills not starting fires

BIO

Day of alarm and despond
somehow sweet, as in reflected sweet
the wish to assume becoming rages
just as soon as you get better

"The twit," he thinks
It is (is it?) the measure of this fabulous sky
that it reminds me of no other sky
He thinks, "The twit"

His frenzy—or mine—is always
the same

      We correspond
on the matter

        ("It is a state
we normally medicate")

And it is the measure of this frenzy
how far gone you are
when fully relieved

It is a lucky something,
the way he figures it,
that doesn't happen
(given present company)

      II

Some days he remembers
more of what he's read
than others—

                    in fact
        he lives to be remembered
        and remember himself

                    III

        He remembers:
        When the gun goes off
        the music stops
        the crowd thins out
        and if you're in for the long haul
        you'd be wise to do the same

DOGSBODY

Head down
        while he jogs
the memory of a taste,
           a voice
constantly fails to correct
a sleepy need to travel.

Somewhere else
        gives the rest of him
reason to follow
        the old arguments:

Rain out, guts in.

Neon hits
        the wet street
and shakes his bones
           into some commotion...

the voice that calls
        a dead body that remains.

DESCENT FROM GRACE

"Leave!"
Is the chant of the pleased heart
          In the upstart son

Good parents, do not dry
                Lacy, you say?

Lacy, hell! Lacy too!
Hell—
                    Exactly the de riguer reticent
          Palm frond type—

                Beer salvo
Pucked-upon bozo, leer killer—
          A lech neglectful

So young!
Arcane lame now fizzy
                Pouring tea
          On the dot each day

Good parents, do not dry
The champs "So long!" it
                on loonier errands
          Untrue

POEM: TO THE COAST INDIAN

Set these floating microbes off
                                    to a sane distemper
Take the blood back
                        spilled at birth
Speak of something other
                                    than you have ever
spoken of before.

                        "These are the times
the elders spoke of"
                                and you
are simple and finally an expression
of that presently remembered speed

You have come halfway,—
                            near as damnit, anyway

There is a tribe
                    that has to leave to learn
You heard this young—
                            kept it ordinary—
flag in every wind

GOODBYE FOREVER

Shit, I'm busting out of this mill!
Yes, I am! Getting out of this burg!
Leaving! Quitting the place! Splitting!
Making my beat! Making tracks! Hauling out!
Heading out! Hauling ass! Heading elsewhere!
Vacating the premises! Bent on all points other!
Vamoose, I! Picking them up and laying them down!
Following the sun! Moving out! Moving on!
Making for more clement climes! Hauling
These bones out of here! Avanti! Away, me!
Me, I'm fading! Fade me! Changing
My whereabouts! My tune! Relocating!
Taking it on the lam! Beating my feet!
Taking the path of least resistance!
Cashing in my chips! Making a fresh start!
Cutting my losses! Tending west! Heading east!
Packing up my old kit bag! Pulling up the stakes!
Draggin'! Cutting loose! This kid's history!
Watch my smoke! I'm breaking my contract!
Keepin' on keepin' on! Emigrating! Moving
My cookies! Changing the record! Making haste!
Going on the run! Read truckin'
For wistfully sprinting! Shipping out!
Sailing with the tide! Saddling up!
Mounting my nag! Shimmering off! Departing!
Dissembling! Blowing this joint! Disappear!
Making myself scarce! Going off! Remaining not!
Otherwise traipsing! Trotting off! Tripping off!
Shifting off! Wandering off! Oiling out!
Evacuating! Vanishing! Taking myself elsewhere!
Relocating! Generally resettling! Picking up
The Pieces! Casting my fate to the wind!
Setting sail! Setting out! Setting off!

Turning my back on all that once was!
Burning through! Breaking through! Breaking off!
Shuttling forward! Shuffling off! Cutting the cord!
Jumping bail! Shifting my load! Putting in
For a transfer! Taking it on the road!
Otherwise disposing of myself! Replanting!
Jumping ship! Emptying the coffers! Closing
All accounts! Once since gone! One presently absent!
Aspiring to be no longer among those present!
With us no more! Literally vacuous!
Elsewhere Represented! Fervently without!
Desirous of other office! Sprung! Soon to be
In frequent correspondence with those now present!
Keen maker of the heart grow fonder! Gone
Like a cool breeze! A.W.O.L.! Becoming
Dim-pictured! No longer at this address!
Gone but not forgotten! Author of this goodbye!
Poof! What I'll do is leave! Though known,
Now vague! Obscure! Abstracted! A nameless haze!
I'm packing it in! Tossing my lot! Casting off!
Cruising through! Disporting anew! Newly moved!
The new hand! New kid on the block! Prominent loss!
Mr. Tootle-oo! Go-go bozo! I'll be shoving off!
Shifting gears! Shagging out! Taking off
For parts unknown! In fact, taking off!
Flying the coop! Taking care of a few last details!
I'm the one winkled away on or about this day!
I'm out of here! Kicking up dust! Dearest, I wish
You the best of everything and shall watch your future career
With considerable interest! Off I go! Skeedadle!
Flying away! Grabbing a cab! Giving up my chair!
Gone globe-trotting! Soon to present a letter
Of introduction! Sending love to his and her people!
Presuming significant distance! Doing a bolt!
Conspicuous in my absence! Having a wonderful time!
End of transmission! Sayonara! Adios!
Au revoir! Aloha! So long!

SONG

The world will curl up
The world will curl your remarkable lip
And if you live forever if, quip well, abiding time
Abides
And seizing time flies to seasons of will
and want.

          Lended phonic semblance
Rents promotion of the flesh.
It is widespread lesser bucks
Swipes delight,
                         and general flight
Hobbles noted passage rites.
It is massively same and seeming brief
But gasp-lastly right.

                    It is a song
Of sorts of usual and triumphant nature.

OLD YEAR

An enormous cordial,
Explosive and able
Driving out the year—
The train rolls by
Behind our heads
Late in the valley bottom night.

In December I get scared
And haul my weekly resent
Of the fleet up with me—
Finding merit, gone by
Or upcoming, in another year,
In the sound of struck brass
Or, easily, mentioned ocean.

In November I wonder
All the same.
I wonder the same.
Incessant as a rainstorm
In a book, the physically strong
Woman moves in and right out
Of a good friend's life.

Facts shorten with the days.
Proper names swarm at year's end.
Old ideas of time, forever untried,
Appear less tired.
Awful, we say, awful...
But the comfort is slight
In something soon foolish.

And the feel of leaving,
Often strong, is shot
By the thought :
"I'll name my kid Chad,"
Or a similar note
Floating in pages and pages
Of decade superstitions.

It is an open-ended dread—
Best met traveling, in stable waiting,
Or stunned with numerous local papers
Flat on the back.

DRYSDALE AND MANTLE, WHITEY FORD AND TO YOU

Wet snow falling on no snow
Go on over and ask her to dance
then we'll toast the old bastards
and shut this gathering up

There is precious little
between bites
but it is hard to lightly bite
loved ones
for thinking of dead ones

That man's joy, that woman's joy
comes to us
not so much in similar words
– quote or coincidence–
but I think in lethal duet
vowel train, crossword puzzle whim
– a flick of the scat-capable wig

The man I am thinking of
is—good God—hereabouts

and this is the Last Call he heard
from the day he was born—O Ted!

THE ISLANDS

How armored folk fear chase
Well prepared days
And the faltering pin
Lands unseen or pretty near
Linen sands such as these
In a quiet room

A hag came to quench
The white on the wall
A-hearing her and all
My things considerately
Renouncing rounds and wiles
Noise and pain

Too long, and quick to scatter woe
I was seventy-seven
No more human than warm
I shall shortly be too often
Seen another age

To that peace I swear
A ghastly birth

For when you come to skirts of lawn
Passing tied, manners to issues
As in Sundays, moon-phases, dawns
To what you got to kneel beside
Female dusts will burgeon
Clutter and bind these hard lands
Where their song shall keep

THE BROWNS

Bowing to the nouns (they are)—
sizable in number and stuck
in their sides and sizes,
the perimeter of their wit…

Over dinner, the fish split in half—
a horrifying franchise to each—
brings on the talk, but often
hardly. Still, they see no real
difficulty—slow-going or otherwise.

Rest them would be the prayer
of the well-intentioned but uninformed.

MRS MURCHESON

Her heart was the warmer
for she was lovely.
She as white like a sonnet
in evening gray not premature.
Unskilled at what she would confer
five afternoons, every moment matter snow.
Many men in services.
She gave them bright quiets—
she felt you should,
quickly and surely, each humbly.
She practice, singing "two by two,"—
ambled down a street,
gave it war-relief organization
where she looked. She had come
stopping, kept thanking, thanking.
Individually, the design, a uniform,
eked near, but the idea
was necessarily far. Still,
with a fuller shirt and a long friend maybe…
She stops—fog's halted—then whistles.
Light's on. Let's go. Light's on.

BASIN DAYS

A sound felicitation straight away
Pegged his light right by the spire
Abrupt in plants at dark

We had assessed from an earlier lanai
Courting sectors later with the Olds
While, brochure-perfect, proxy fakes
Behaved, and toured the points
Famed in umber vistas
Home, to go to, lavished holes
Upon the sanctuary bulletins
The "favorite (blank)" within
Harboring calms of lots, essentials
Now more scarce than rarely the reminders
They had been, let alone those
Rhymes of Dad's

I go ahead and dump

Past aspects, mated, bake
And it is fortunate, for once, that
Even in deliveries of the best of
Annual plans, one finds
No curious mode

Just what gaze was it, then
Made it known?—suspect among fixtures
As, and meaning it, who isn't?

Finding places for things
From other places, stopping that
To start this, then rushing

To be part or piece, glaze or taint or glint,
You name it, spangle

Or say, the clutch in these
Quicker, more elaborate type
Developments—they haul ass

Vinnie!

Ditch

Days away present...careful
(I still have the shirt)
No phone
Invisible with hours

39, 40, 50, a dollar
Come Again

Meanwhile, a fluttering of clues
Rounds up the part of the fact
Lost and antic facets—*yoo-hoo!*—here
To be included with his friends
By name in the level assembly

My space, knit then
Amidst responses to a common sequence
To date continues aft

Finishing up, I sleep

O sanction, bear your beneficent gate
To facing these squirrelly verbs
Sweatless in my place
Dear, dear gate

I awoke at the first promotion
Noting flows
Bent on making sense
Err, bent on mention

P.S. Enclosed please find
My letter of intent and sketches

A constant stoppage readied our surprise
Which, something of a flood, would
Bash the whole cast into walls
Or some sort of aftermath, at least, like
A brand new day of the week, up, aiming

May we help you?

Actually, the most recent readings
Still, as yet, cannot impart
A total stack, as it were
Toward any single one sudden

Who, thought, 's counting?
Who would rather a calendar of conditions?

After unmitigated, didn't we all score poppycock?

Perhaps the explanation for this
Loitering of results, if such
Is the case, may be near
And not back at an, afterall, determined
Start—right here
Within the regimen up front
The crates we think of
During lunch

Just watch the lock
Unholster some pre-something
Of the cave, now, watch

Daylight-saving time
Flu
The Hop

Yesterday, yes
Today, no

Try to sleep

The according marks the start (*oops!*)
A hobby of mine, sort of
Thought not so much in title
As the half, passing
The line down the middle
Of a national example

Now...Off, drunk strummer
He opens, lights the sign
Further up, at last, the first
Checks through, moves

There is more, I tell you, than just
Our hints and selves, assorted stats
And so forth, to these trailing shapes
A mist, for one, would more than venture
Flatter passage

The differences, in fact, actually
Make tents and shade, all that
And for a very long time
I, for one, remain

ALL RIGHT BY ME

I'm just going to sit right here
You go on ahead
Without me
I'm fine
Thanks, no, I don't want a thing
I'll just stay where I am
Don't you worry about me
Everything's just fine
Really
Couldn't be better
I don't want to see a movie
I've seen a movie
Yes, the day looks gorgeous
Out the window
I must insist, though
Not another thing
Not another word
Everything is jake
All right by me
I'm just going to sit right here

AEROSPACE

In great secrecy, at first light,
the air craft rose and rotated fifty miles southwest,
gently lifting its nose to fly.
Conditions were good: firmly humid,
but not so near the coastal plain.

No sound...The propeller sank rapidly
onto a small fenced field...the rest
another place. Leaves covered up
its nose. Hung still, the prop
was a full half mile away.

A few runs without horizon...
This black flat land...And today...
It's data. Data where no activity was,
and modern for that. Data gathered,
colored bright. Flags

                      "We want

motion from tall poles
in the wind."

ABOUT POETRY (II)

for Keith Abbott

Railing disclaimers sass the aging flights
that, lost in a line, need their call
to recount.

                  But dizzy hailing worthies
I am light—I think I'm light—and toss
these options aft.

             Next the line
lights at the child, and is applauded.

Next my harm in time is charming.

I'm a dummy in the sun...
                  or (worse) someone
louder once...
             or a sucker for a train song
in a train song.

Take a page...
             come up busy and empty...
left to right, black and white.

CALLING S.J. PERELMAN

Begging your pardon, ma'am, and meaning no harm by it I'm sure
       But have you with all respect lost your mind?
No! No police! You promised! Speak up when you talk to me, boy...
       Nothing to be afraid of here. I see it,
But I don't believe it! Your honor, I object, counsel
       for the defense is attempting to turn this courtroom
into a three-ring circus. I own everything in this town
       worth owning but the post office and the phone company
and I'm working on that, so you think very careful the next time
       you've got an urge to rattle my cage, boy.
Nurse! Get this patient an I.V. stat and give me more suction!
       Colonel, I did not come 3,000 miles
over some of the most desolate, God-forsaken territory
       ever seen by mortal man just to hear your views
on the growing Indian problem! You may kiss the bride
       That's the last time I loan him twenty dollars,
I'll tell you that much. For heaven's sake, Arthur, I said
       a *small* dog! Rio at last! This is a business,
Mr. Havermeyer, not a charity organization. The last time
       I was here I was no bigger than you are now, son.
No daughter of mine is going to her first cotillion at the club
       in some...some...jalopy! No response yet
from the Kremlin, Mr. President. He may not be a big shot
       on Wall Street with a big fancy chauffeur-driven car...
not yet anyway...but I love him and he loves me and we're going to
       get married tomorrow morning at nine o'clock and that's that!
I don't understand, it was here a minute ago. Sorry, Johnny,
       I'm going to have to take you downtown.
The difference is, Baron, he is loved by the people...You are feared
       by them. We have gathered together here
the greatest minds of our time, the foremost experts from every field
       and discipline of the physical and metaphysical sciences

and set before them one unifying goal: to save the world!

    I'm afraid I could not possibly accept a bet of this size
without first checking with the manager. Truth be told,

    she dumped me. 'Pon my soul, Cletis,
little Mable's growed all up into a fine figure of a girl...

    Damned if she ain't.

FEVER

for Alice Notley

I have just made a movie with Sammy Davis, Jr.,
and there are three crumpled dollar bills
on an old wooden post for me. I pick them up
and see there is also a ten dollar bill.
I pick that up to buy a Cremolata Italian ice
from an old man in an enormous straw hat.
He gives me the ice but says he can't change the ten
and returns it. This ten, though, is a different ten
of deep red rust colors around the edges and a picture
of Mrs. Wallace Stevens in a lawn chair. Joe Carioca,
the Walt Disney parrot (or like-looking bird),
is actually suddenly there beside me, high up
on a very tall post. He is dressed in a full-blown
Gay Caballero outfit including a colorful cape
and black seven league pirate boots. Joe Carioca
tells me that bills like the funny ten I just got
were issued during the war in Key West
and the Virgin Islands and that they are now
very rare and worth a fortune. Furthermore,
he tells me he knows where to exchange them.
Mrs. Wallace Stevens comes to life and hears this.
Another Key West/Virgin Islands bill shows up
(this time a hundred dollars), indicating the presence
of many more war-issued bills. We're in the money!
I say to Mrs. Wallace Stevens, "Do you hear
the beating of the drums?"—meaning island native drums
and the approach of wild good times of tropical excess
and fleshy splendor. She says, "Yes! and a new dress!"
We set off at once to locate our guiding parrot
who has since disappeared. Eventually we did find him,
though, snagged upside-down in a fishnet—
the very method Mrs. Wallace Stevens and myself
had decided to use to capture that extraordinary bird.

POEM

Quick, into the almanac!
Whip the cloth
From under the plates and vase
It is green all around
A person may be truly able
While he waits
And don't we wait
In service to the past
In aid of beauty
You just don't <u>know it</u>
The sources are not just revealed
It's not as though you don't know this, though
I'm pulling forgotten numbers
Out of the old air
They are threadbare
But may provide a song
Ain't it going to be empty
When they've left!

COLORADO

Shadow takes the butte
Rolls across the valley floor
Works up the facing hillside
Many birds squabble by two white chairs
High up, easy winds pretty the clouds
Bird handbook does me no good at all

Jack Collom, somewhere in this state
Would specify every fussin' one
Not long ago, one bird, gold and black
Hopped up and paused on the white chair
Jack would be sitting in
Were Jack here.

THE LITIGANTS

Begged to demand/beware emphatic change
I will never sleep again
"That will do"
Turn to the wind–anything
That prevails when simply present

Gaze at the cars
Sitting in the sun out the open door
I am awake to be reminded
Of other cars in another light
Out another open door

You are too
(As in Who isn't?)

Or you. Did you ever
Get that letter?

The sky sighs
And settles on your shoulders
You may speak

Morning in this world
Friday in the spring
The two of them together
They watch in the water
In each a rhythmic adjustment is made

"Everyone is haunted
Watch the water"

When the light is right
Everything means it
Spring's first peach pit
In the ashtray

"You've got a lot of nerve!"
Amen
May I be excused?

City Starless night
The sky goes orange
In the trail of the advancing rain.

POEM

She holds the bird a minute to her lips
Before returning it, weary, home:
Something signal and fine
With more than a bit of the randier ads
And hence, as I dreamed it, a sense of people
Having died in the name of the sentiments
They contained. We have forfeit
The requirement of our consent.
We begin to hear more than we'd wished.
Now, again, she is damned and appropriate.
"Bitchin' kamikazee ingenue" is right
(singing, "Do wah diddy, diddy dum diddy do")
Like the guys who followed the birds south
Laying down a railroad along their path—
Stunts recalling amphetamines' exacting perfidy
(Now grown sweet) or even, more recently,
Engaged in locating subatomic deities,
Perhaps merely standing, greatly, by.
From a walk to a halt to a walk—
What it amounts to. And so
Back out into the customary air
Turning her face to her sources.

THIN AIR

Convinced, I verb the modern stop,
I relinquish heritage tidal sighs
For those more complete at command

A splendid confusion pre-empts
All I make:
The will and the wish—I don't know!
I am so happy neglecting
The station to decide!

Outside the heat conspires to reside,
And by that alone all movement
Must have noise. My voice
In bickering incidents—
All contrary to direction, all
Some other rote.

Motion in heat, on a grass now lawn
And dying, could well be
Impossible from here....

I am in spite of my life.
I sort and die. I die talking.

RARITY PLANES

L.A. Or As A

thin sleep between the vital spansules say
or an ice cream sandwich here in a
midst without middle

75 degrees in the middle of March

You find nothing but
introductions to what you doubtless
would have met anyway

"Some sweltering ides for the missus, fella?"

I am ceaselessly invited
And there is never an attempt to entice
– a huge trust without affection
for accidents
                Hence, I think,
Las Vegas, Reno, up the state (and over)—
their numbers portraying me
on the felts of what I just now tried to dream

Yet the random's had it

I find myself hungry when I shouldn't,
horny as I boff, Also:
Faithful to the sound of myself
as I have explained it there,
                    or am here
in a journal I never will nor want to own
but have on occasions visited @
12 bucks a throw

Had it

　　　And another charge is inexplicably induced
into the roiling blood
I am offered the memory of a pregnant cat
in someone's pregnant cat,
　　　　　　　　the stink,
especially, of summer kittens in a kitchen box
in a weather mocking weather

　　　　　　　　　　"Some uh..."

but as if the intellect at last
had present senses—half a dozen
generations spent gone catapulting memory
home at last

　　　　* * *

Or am I mocking myself?

Or am I an immediate echo?

One thing—
　　　　　　there is no doubt
I would ask these questions
Ask David Sandburg, ask Bill Bathhurst

Should you, really,
　　　　　　or
do I want to be remembered there
as I'm remembered here?

I am grateful for these dilemmas

Still not because they can never really be
in practice here which here it is is
why I came

                        I am grateful for the asking
I am pure fashion, Elvis Presley,
or all of that decade I cannot recall,
but which I am sure was the truer founding
of the midst its grey so tickling

That, but never slick
as this decade would say, 'said self consciously,'
never so popping fresh atta-boy stalk a stalk whew
as at times admitted wont

only full of words

in the absence of a childhood
which I mourn have mourned am mourning
as a primitive
                        – whole fiestas
great pips ah spizzle
                                    of an olden whoop-by-god
captioning the original thigh-slap

                        * * *

Find me that way as you can find me
giggling as you do
because I know how you know me
because you have known me before
(why *you* came)—
                        a dash for fitting
as we our decade peruse the welcoming steads
in space

In space?
               Absolutely.
We haven't got a chance of anywhere else.
We have made space in denying it
(like here, thinking "stars" or "outer")
as we have denied its puns, savvy?

We could go on forever doing it too
but we won't,
                              because we just
aren't comfortable when we forget
what it all once

                    * * *

For example knowing the house of my childhood
was once an orange or lemon grove
has often kissed, flattered, me to death, sleep
And I can think of nothing better to do
when such things matter

They are mattering, apparently, now
I can't fall asleep
and I haven't yet told you the picture that got me up from trying

...a random cup, tripped empty on the carpet

                    * * *

But here the nerves are regardless,
like Heaven, a dare
I can't eat my sandwich now but
there isn't any stuff—Glad Bags, foil
and the same with my tea, poor steeping,
                                        we

are all going respectively dry, cold,
cold—my back hurts
and a girl is sighing at the light

But too, I seem to be enjoying it
natch—hot during the day
cold at night—nerves and slow-talk,
titter and dread, fears of sleep (trying),
fears of not—all in me mind you

Dares, if you wish,
beneath the Broadway Tower

...splash gong the Wilshire sidewalk

I've never thought of it
but I know someone who has

Later I went to the museum
and looked at myself looking in the glass
over Robert Motherwell's *Acrobatic Wave*—
which I have been meaning to mention, someplace,
for some time
                        as it was the first dare

(example—not in particular,
but nature, tone—:
                        Find the lie
in that stanza. Or this stanza, for that matter.)

Robert Motherwell, your wave's regardlessness
was a promise then
                        A promise
was a dare,
                        though to what, of what
exactly, I can't exactly say

Nor can I say if that mattered
(upon the air regarding) (me not the wave)

Anyway an illustration—
an attitude so (looked something
like this ➤) attentive it was blind

– That's not it. But I do like the way it sounds,
and later what it implies

...an attitude so complete it never knew it

....Nor can I really be sure it was
there, as far as you-to-me
is concerned in any of the great ways
it can and cannot be

                              If it was an accident
we are both geniuses of emulation (of accidents)

...an impersonation so total it was new
– strictly,—born, new—not the ruin
built-upon or revamped old

which is absolutely everything else:

"I love being in your poems"
and:
"Why aren't I in any of your poems?"

....But I don't really think
either one of us are the type
for any kind of totality, or that word
for ultimate I can't think of

                                        ('plasms of quick-light
across my eyes, teeth ache now as well),—

not judging by our previous
                                and subsequent works, no

Da-dum

                        * * *

In the meantime we had Easter
I was out walking, weighing prickly pears
and then not, walking by the Convalescent Center
on Eighth Street, then Ninth
and I watched all the drapes pulled open,
windows, we were getting better
or worse, knowing it, as we frequently do,
but choosing this day, a little more
than incidental, to say it to someone else
who was or wasn't getting the same

You see, we never really did believe
that he came back to life

But isn't it enough that all those people
wanted him to? some probably before he died?

I would have loved to've been alive then
never asking that

                        And this, I think,
is this more than a wish because it has never
been promised me?

Stupid question.

But you know that in asking,

                                        who cares what,

I was afraid of something.

Who cares what?

On the other hand this isn't prose
altho it looks like it here by hand
(first writing by hand in a long time)

                                        which damn

doesn't sound at all like it should
(it's the 'on the other hand...'),

                        like it means

I am grateful for the asking
I appreciate the manner most—

assuming 2000 years ("of bad beer
and worse onions")

                        no,

of never-say-die cool and frantic
straight down the line purports

They're there without me, I mean it

but no one ever said purports for reasons
manner for style

                        just because he's heard it,

and I...

am Elvis Presley

That's fear

I'm fear.
                    This isn't a marathon
It is the unveiling of an exceptional
and highly disturbing sensibility

                              (he said it sensibility!)

"of our time"

I'm not

I am better than TV because like my children
I don't care if you believe me
(if you aren't all of you)
(where are you...now?

                         are you awake, in bed?)

which also isn't it,
                "though I do like..."

I am not unlike TV because,
more so than of your belief,
I care for your watching

                    Hence everything
I talk about sounds,
as a friend of mine put it not the one who thought of 'it' earlier,
like I am talking about myself

Well, I didn't kiss him,
                    but I would have
if he hadn't said it to me

Quote, are you
just going to sit there make riddles all night
or what?

Now he
would be the one I didn't kiss
because he make him a she probably wouldn't
kiss me back

         – something that hasn't happened in years
as far as I know...

            "Come on, relax—have some more punch."
            "Oh fuck off."

        * * *

I changed my mind: I want you to believe me

Then I want you to ask me how come
Then I want to be eccentric and do something like not answer you
or something (due to my mood)
Then I want you to look up why how come (why how come) someplace
in this poem

        * * *

I changed my mind: don't bother
It's too late. I think something is at hand

I want you to ask me how come
                because
it would mean you were afraid and American

This is part of it.
        It isn't much, but,
if you're willing, is enough.
We'll start from there

        (Footnote: three octaves—no—four octaves

below the above falsetto guised
below the above falsetto guised:

We all like a little respect now and again

"Riddlemonger!"

There is much to be said for being feared, or respected)

        * * *

I don't want to start. I'm afraid now,
really afraid

"Crazy patriot!"

No, no—stop it. I don't want to be clever at all.
I want to have arrived, by boat,
just a week ago,
              and making
great progress with the language...

      Americans are a fearful people. They are separate
in groups because they are not separate in themselves.
They share a language, now, not a land. (There are
more words for group than there are for soil or sen-
sation.) Because of this an attitude spoken may for
some be anarchy, for others cliché.
      Yes they keep talking....It is a wonderful party.
Not only did they earn the right to talk but, more
modern, the right to talk what they are talking about.
      Then someone laughs at it with his friends.
      They are resented at once....How did they get
in here?
      And they are resented at once.

There is no more distancing sentiment. It too is modern, and is easily distorted and denied, or disbelieved, because of its lack of history.

I am what you are not afraid of but should be. Personally, I would rather you fear me than fear you myself because I am the one who knows it is easy. It really is easy.

POEM

Oh, Mom, it is so beautiful

ACKNOWLEDGMENTS

Some of these poems appeared in the following books:

Smith Going Backward, San Francisco: Cranium Press, 1968.
Fleur-de-Lis, San Francisco: Blue Suede Shoes VII, circa late 60s.
Gentle Subsidy, Bolinas: Big Sky, 1975.
The Lily of St. Marks, New York: "C" Press, 1978.
The California Papers, New York: United Artists, 1981.
AP, New York: Archipelago Books, 1984.
20 Poems, New York: Unimproved Editions Press, 1987.

20 Poems was reprinted by Open 24 Hours in 2006. The editor wishes to thank the publishers of these books as well as the editors of the numerous small magazines and journals that printed and supported Steve's work over the years. Some of those include: *Angel Hair, Best & Company, Big Sky, Blue Suede Shoes, The Cheap Review of Poetry, The Paris Review, Roots Forming, Vice, The World, Yale Literary Magazine* and the anthologies *Another World, Up Late: American Poetry Since 1970,* and *The World Anthology.*

The editor also wishes to thank Marion Farrier, Joseph Carey, Tom Carey, Elinor Nauen, Lytle Shaw, Keith Abbott, Alice Notley, Simon Pettet, John Coletti, Greg Fuchs, and Anselm Berrigan for their support in making this book happen.

Steve Carey was born in Washington DC in 1945, and published seven collections of poetry before his death in 1989. "Steve", an essay on his life and writing, can be found in Alice Notley's *Coming After: Essays on Poetry*. This selected poems is the first book in over twenty years to make Carey's work widely available.